BRAIN TwiSTeRs

3D HOW IT WORKS

Two pictures are printed overlapping each other, one in red and the other in green. When viewed through your amazing 3D glasses you will see a stereoscopic picture that leaps off the page. This is how it works. One color is absorbed and may become invisible. For example, if you look at red and green lines through a red filter, only the green lines will be visible – they will appear to be black. When the two superimposed images are viewed with your 3D glasses, one eye sees the green image and one eye sees the red image. This is a stereoscopic view. Now you can look at images as though they were three dimensional.

Although initially developed for entertainment, there are many serious applications for 3D photography, which is highly sophisticated. 3D is used in map making, medical/surgical photography, and space exploration.

If you are patient, the special 3D images in this book will amazingly rise up off the page when viewed through the 3D glasses supplied (red lens left, green lens right). If you turn the glasses around and look again, the images will appear to retreat! Test your brain power now with these bamboozling visual challenges.

Here is a picture of a young lady – or is it of her grandmother? If you can't see both women, try making the young girl's chin become her granny's nose. Drawn by W.E.Hill, this was first published in 1915.

Am∆zing MAGIC

KITE FLYING SPECTACULAR

Using your 3D glasses, can you work out which number tail belongs to which kite on the opposite page?

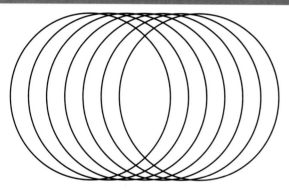

Left: Rotate the page in a counterclockwise direction to make the wheels on the bicycle spin

GOING ROUND IN CIRCLES!

"Flip-flop" images can appear to change direction. Does the tube below have its front opening on the left or right? ...

... and is this a cone or a tunnel?

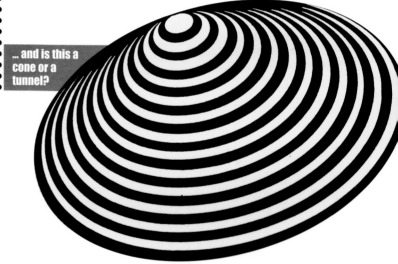

Look at the spiral below. It isn't a spiral at all, but a series of circles. Check it out with a compass if you're not convinced!

Rotating this page vigorously will make the circles in this design appear to spin one way with the central cog spinning in the opposite direction!

A A B B C C D D E E F F G G H H I I J J

1 1 2 3 4 4 5 5 6 6 7 7 8 8 9 9 10 10

AmaZing MAGIC

COUNTING CONUNDRUMS

GOING UNDERGROUND

Using your 3D glasses start at the top of the page. Can you find a route that will take you to the end of the line marked by a circle at the bottom of the page? You are not allowed to change trains. That means you have to stay at the same level all the way.

There is another route that will take you to the bottom of the page, but not to the end of the line − can you find that as well?

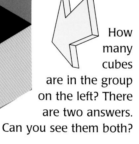

How many cubes are in the group on the left? There are two answers. Can you see them both?

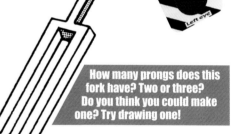

How many prongs does this fork have? Two or three? Do you think you could make one? Try drawing one!

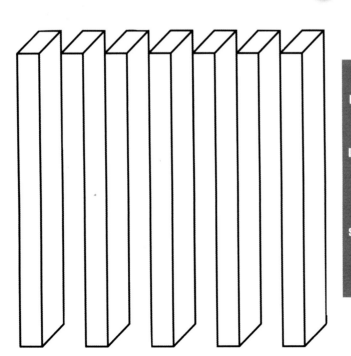

How many planks are in the picture on the left? Is it seven? Or is it five?

These two spirals look identical. One is made from one line and the other from two. Can you work out which is which?

AMAZING MAGIC

DISTORTED VIEW?

Are the shorter lines in this picture straight? or are they bent? find out for yourself using a ruler or any straightedge.

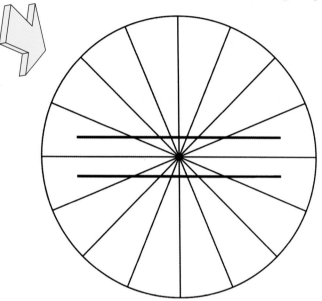

How strange. These four planks seem bent but the salesman assured me they are straight and true!

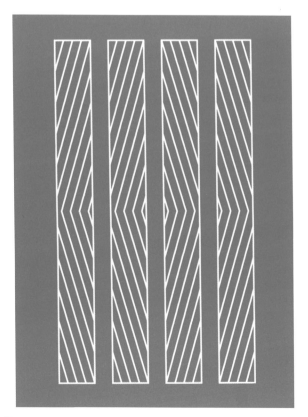

CROSSED PHONE LINES

Using your 3D glasses, view these telephone lines. They are in a real tangle!
Can you unravel them?
Each letter is connected to a number – sort them out to stay connected.

The sides of the square in the circles appear to be bent. Check them out with your ruler.

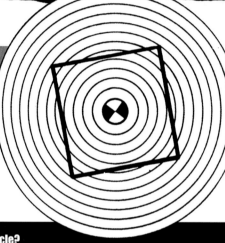

Which dot is in the center of the circle? The yellow one? or the black one?

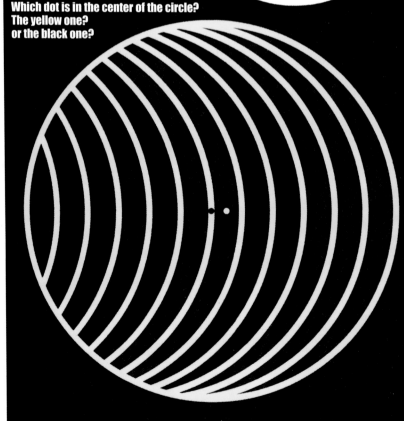

8

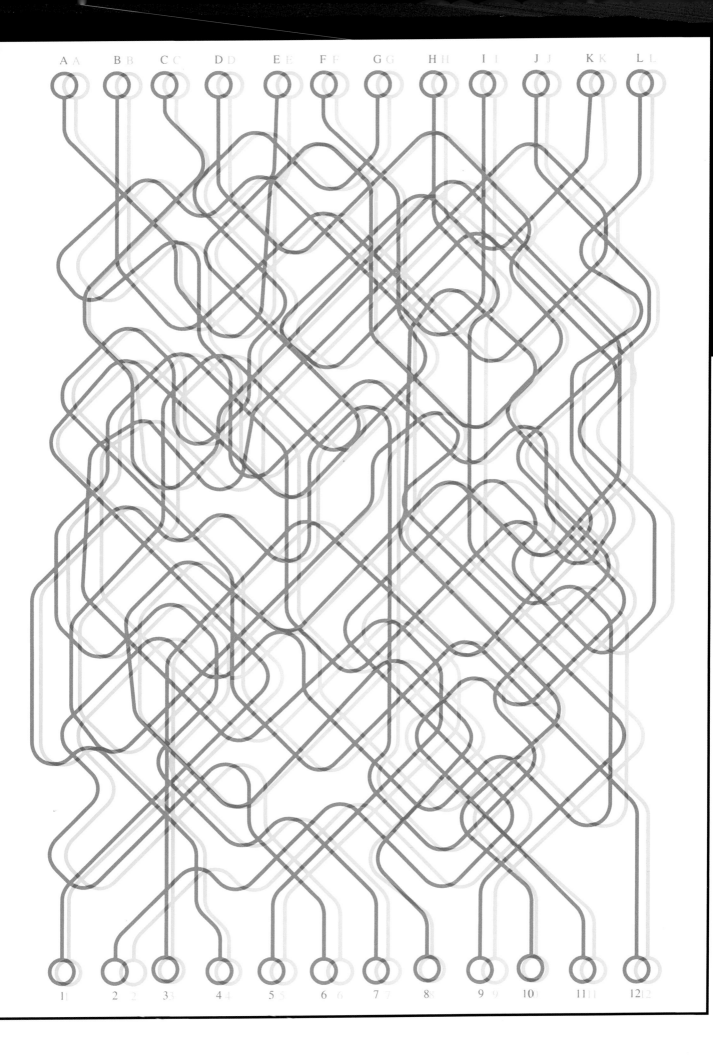

This cube is weird. Can you see other cube shapes in the center of this design?

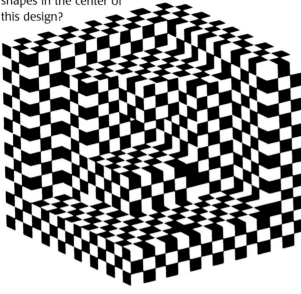

CRYSTAL BALL QUEST

Put on your 3D glasses to view floating steps leading to a crystal ball. From the top of the page which steps will you take to claim the crystal? Have you got it? If you're out of breath, don't worry, there's a shorter escape route to the bottom of the page – if you can find it!

DON'T BE SQUARE!

Look at the group of squares on the left. Can you see mysterious grey spots appearing between the green boxes?

The pattern below may look rather thrown together. View the design at eye level to see how neat they really are!

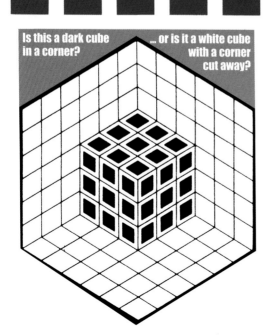

Is this a dark cube in a corner?

... or is it a white cube with a corner cut away?

AMAZING MAGIC

FEELING WOBBLY!

Are the long slanting lines in this design an equal distance apart? Measure with a ruler to find out.

The letters here are all upright even though they might look slanted. Hold the page at arm's length and squint, or view from 13ft (4m) away to get another reading.

Which ends of these two striped bars is the closer, left or right?

BATTLE STATIONS

Put on your 3D glasses and go up step by step to find th shortest route to the battlements at the top of the castle. Warning: do not jump from one staircase to another – th drop could be fatal!

The stripes inside the circles are perfectly horizontal, although you may think they slope towards the center

Is this higgledy-piggledy stack of tiles perfectly even? Check with a ruler or straightedge to find out.

MISSION IMPOSSIBLE!

STEPPING STONES

Use your 3D glasses to move through the maze opposite. Start at the arrow and make your way to a big circle in the middle of the maze. Do not change levels because you might fall into the bottomless pit!

Impossible designs by Oscar Reutersvard, illustrated on these postage stamps issued in Sweden 1982.

Do you think the framework on the left would be possible to make?

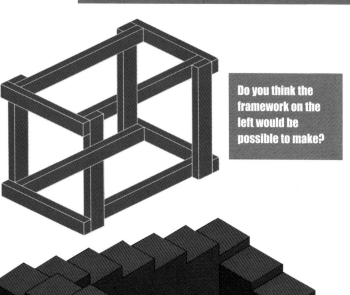

How long before you reach the top step in this staircase?

Impossible building blocks, stars and floating boxes. Just stare at this image to see them all.

14

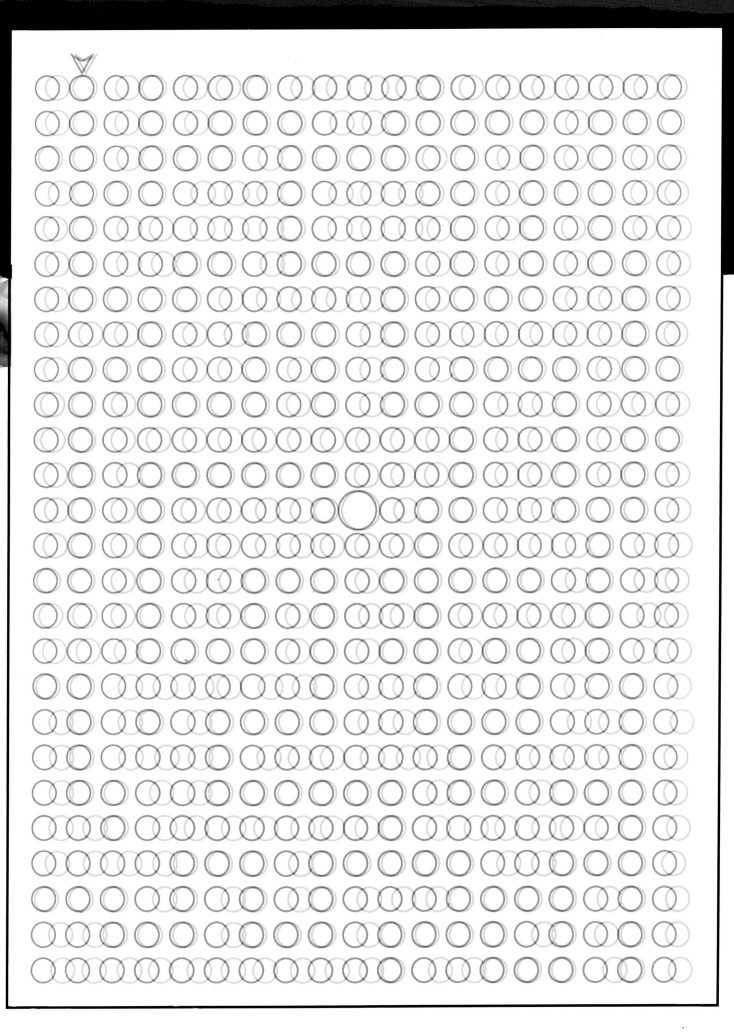

SIZE THESE UP!

Is the wizard greater than the magician or, the magician greater than the wizard? Measure to find out!

STICKY SITUATION

Now, here's a difficult one! Put on your 3D glasses and look at these sticks from above. Starting from the uppermost, try to work out the order in which you could remove each stick without accidentally moving a lower one.

Which pen is the longest? Are you sure? Check them out!

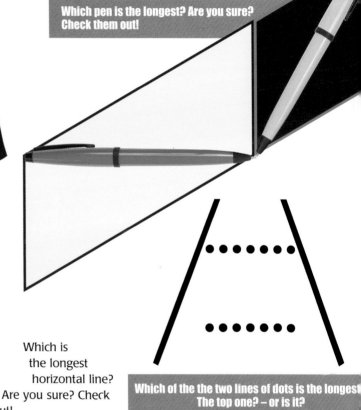

Which is the longest horizontal line? Are you sure? Check them out!

Which of the the two lines of dots is the longest? The top one? – or is it?

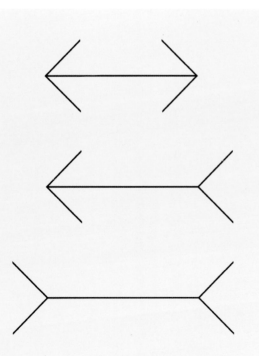

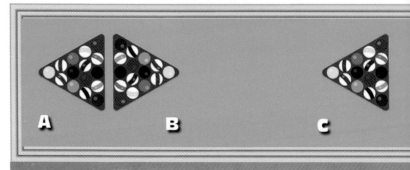

Which distance is greater – A to B or B to C? Use a ruler to find out!

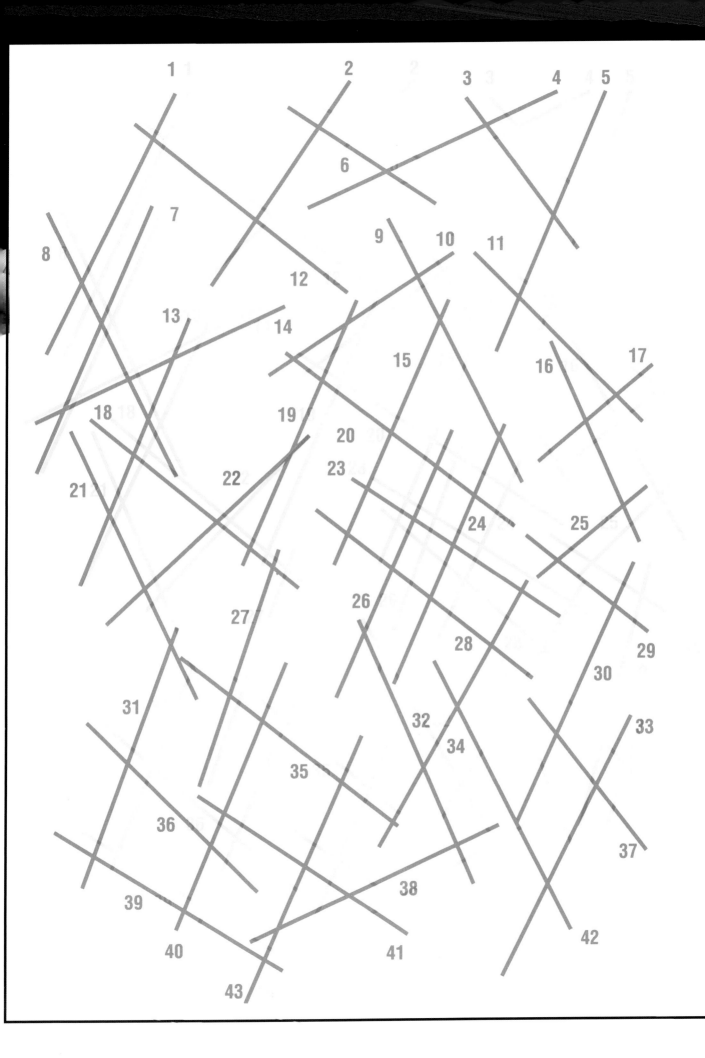

AMAZING MAGIC

MOVING PICTURES

PUZZLING PYRAMIDS

When you put on your 3D glasses to view this puzzle, you will see some of the squares slowly rise until they become pyramids to the gods. The rest will fall into pits of doom. Your challenge is to find the tallest pyramid. This will take a great deal of concentration.

The spiral on the left looks curved, but there are only triangles in this design! No curves! Check it out!

Try staring at this 'Op Art' design by Jean Larcher for a while. Do you find it seems to vibrate and pulse?

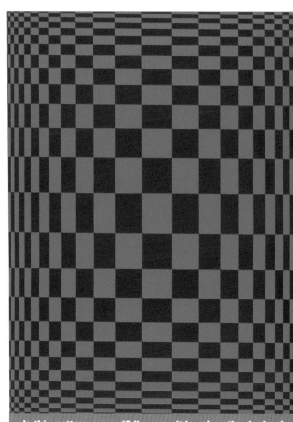

Is this pattern curved? How can it be when the design is made using straight sided rectangles?

DIAMOND DISCOVERY

The Canadian "Maple leaf" flag contains two hidden characters having an argument. Can you find them?

The Old Diamond Mine has one last secret to reveal. Put on your special 3D glasses and descend to the lower levels. Follow the mine workings down and down to unearth the priceless diamond at the center of this amazing mine maze. Now try to escape without dropping the diamond.

HIDDEN FACES

Do you see two blue faces or one yellow candlestick? This classic illusion is known as "The Rubin Vase." ●

These people might have split personalities. Turn the page upside down to see how they change.

Now here's the candle – or is it two more faces?

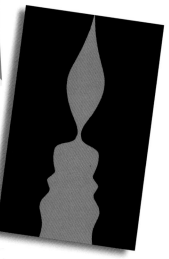

Do you notice anything unusual about this apple core? Look closely and you may see Adam and Eve!

This illusion is seen in newspapers and magazines every day. A series of dots makes up all printed pictures. Look at them close up and they are meaningless. Viewed from a distance the dots change into a halftone photograph.

Am☉Zing MAGIC

ANIMAL MAGIC

THREE DIMENSIONAL GEOMETRIX

The geometric shapes opposite at first seem quite ordinary. Put on your 3D glasses and see the difference stereoscopic vision makes. Now they appear to be fantastic 3D objects floating off the page!

Which way is this bird flying?
Is it flying west or flying east?

How many animals can you see in the woods?
There are actually eight hidden in the branches.

giraffe, lion, camel, elephant, hog, horse, bear and hound

Can you spot the dalmatian dog in the picture below?

Is it a rabbit?
Is it a pelican?
You be the judge.